BUILDING BLOCKS OF PHYSICAL SCIENCE

HEAT

Written by Joseph Midthun

Illustrated by Samuel Hiti

WORLD
BOOK

a Scott Fetzer company
Chicago

World Book, Inc.
180 North LaSalle Street
Suite 900
Chicago, Illinois 60601
USA

For information about other World Book publications,
visit our website at **www.worldbook.com**
or call **1-800-WORLDBK (967-5325)**.
For information about sales to schools and libraries,
call 1-800-975-3250 (United States),
or 1-800-837-5365 (Canada).

Library of Congress Cataloging-in-Publication Data
for this volume has been applied for.

Building Blocks of Physical Science
ISBN: 978-0-7166-4460-6 (set, hc.)

Heat
ISBN: 978-0-7166-4465-1 (hc.)

Also available as:
ISBN: 978-0-7166-4475-0 (e-book)

1st printing March 2022

WORLD BOOK STAFF
Executive Committee
President: Geoff Broderick
Vice President, Editorial: Tom Evans
Vice President, Finance:
    Donald D. Keller
Vice President, Marketing: Jean Lin
Vice President, International Sales:
    Eddy Kisman
Vice President, Technology: Jason Dole
Vice President, Customer Success:
    Jade Lewandowski
Director, Human Resources: Bev Ecker

Editorial
Manager, New Content: Jeff De La Rosa
Associate Manager, New Product:
    Nicholas Kilzer
Sr. Editor: Shawn Brennan
Sr. Content Creator: William D. Adams
Proofreader: Nathalie Strassheim

Graphics and Design
Sr. Visual Communications Designer:
    Melanie Bender
Sr. Web Designer/Digital Media Developer:
    Matt Carrington
Coordinator, Design Development and
    Production: Brenda B. Tropinski
Book Design: Samuel Hiti

Acknowledgments:
Created by Samuel Hiti and Joseph Midthun
Art by Samuel Hiti
Additional art by David Shephard/
    The Bright Agency
Additional spot art by Dreamstime and
    Shutterstock
Text by Joseph Midthun

TABLE OF CONTENTS

There is a glossary on page 39. Terms
defined in the glossary are in type **that
looks like this** on their first appearance.

Hello there!

I'm Heat!

I'm a form of energy that you experience every day!

Have you ever felt the warmth of the sun on your skin?

That sensation you feel...

That's me!

Have you ever sat around a fire? Nice and toasty, right?

If you get too close, you might get burned.

But there's a lot more to me than that!

I'm an important part of your life. In fact, I'm inside your body right now.

Your body creates heat when it uses food.

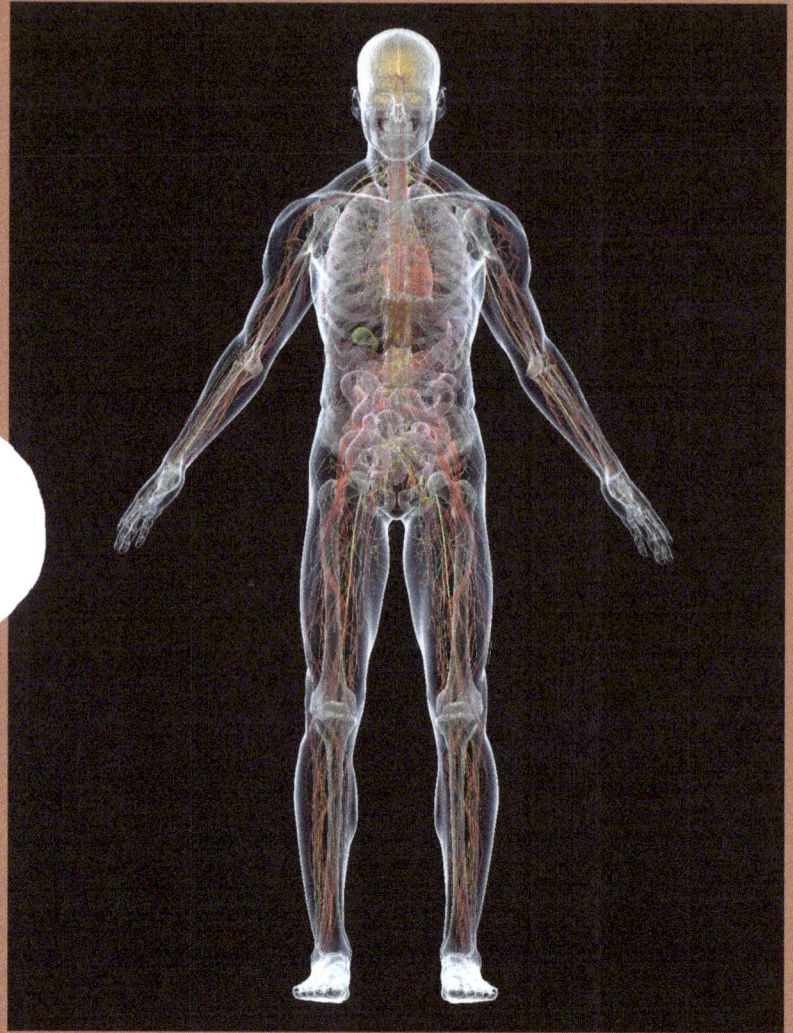

That's how you maintain a steady temperature.

Heat can also be used to power machinery, like this car engine.

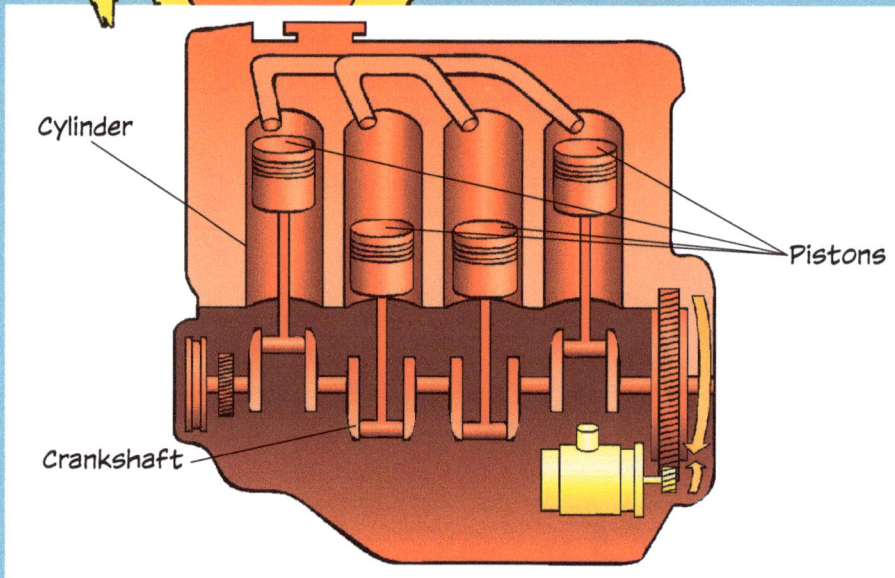

Cylinder

Pistons

Crankshaft

Did you know that the heat from burning fuels provides the power to move nearly all automobiles and airplanes?

Any machine that burns fuel uses heat.

Heat is even used to drive giant machines that make electric power.

Electric power runs everything from lights to toasters to computers.

So you see, heat is being used all around you!

The sun is Earth's most important source of heat.

Life on Earth could not exist without heat from the sun.

Earth also has its own internal heat.

Earth is made up of layers of hot rock and metal.

Volcanoes, hot springs, and geysers all release heat from inside the planet.

Fires and electricity are other sources of heat.

You can also create heat by rubbing two objects together.

All **matter** is made up of tiny moving particles.

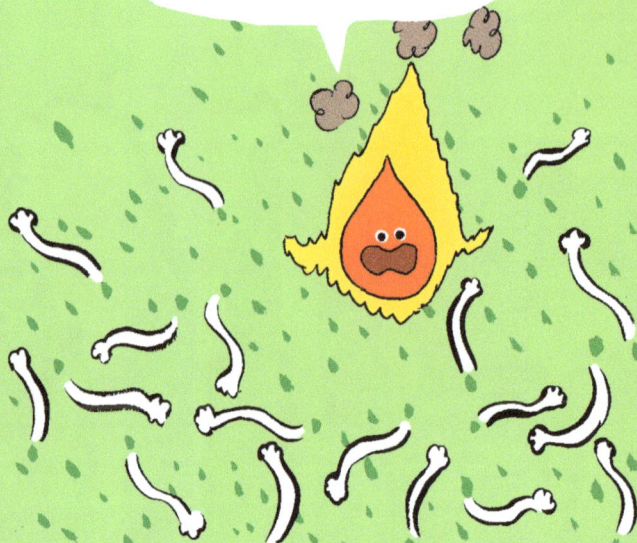

The energy that makes them move is called **thermal energy**.

THERMAL ENERGY

When we heat matter, the thermal energy in its particles increases.

WOOF!

The more energy the particles have, the faster they move.

ZIP

ZIP

ZIP

ZIP

ZOOM

12

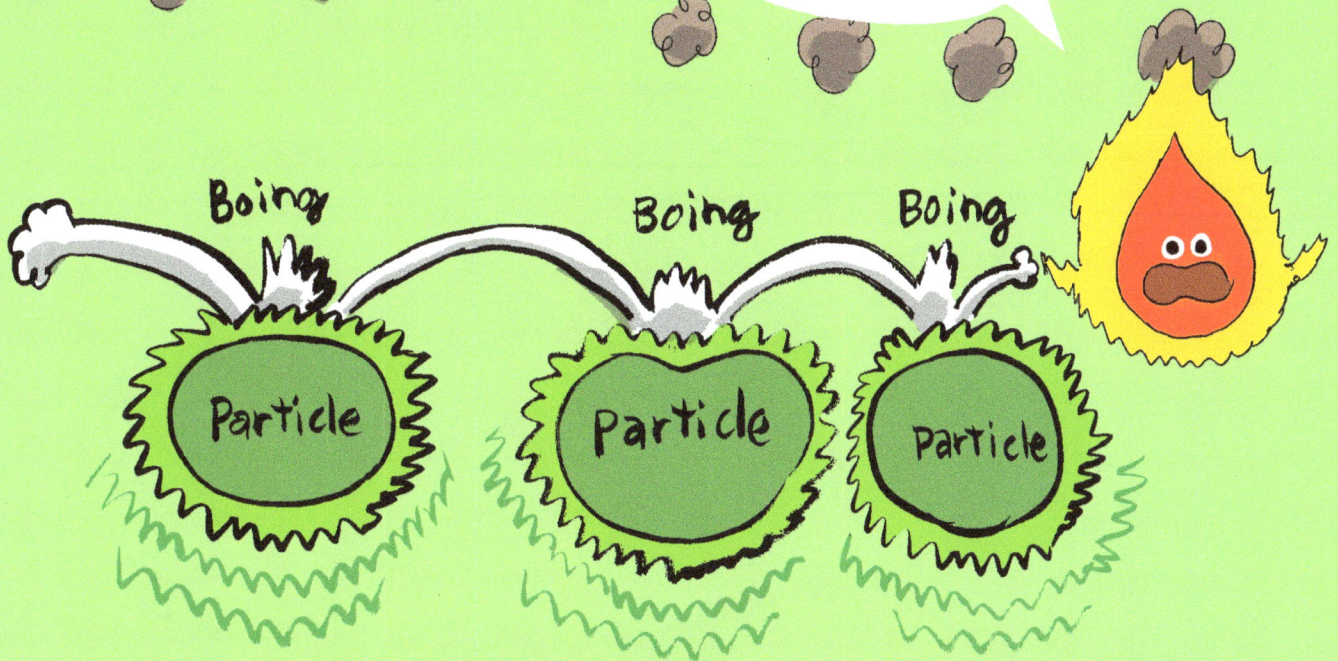

Heat always flows from warmer objects to cooler objects.

I *never* flow from cooler objects to warmer ones.

Let's look at how heat moves in a glass of ice water.

SPLASH

Boing

Boing Boing Boing

The particles in the ice are moving slowly.

The liquid water is warmer than the ice, so its particles are moving a little faster.

The thermal energy from the liquid water flows to the ice.

Then the particles in the ice speed up.

This causes the ice to melt.

It changes from a solid to a liquid.

Eventually, all the water in the glass becomes the same temperature.

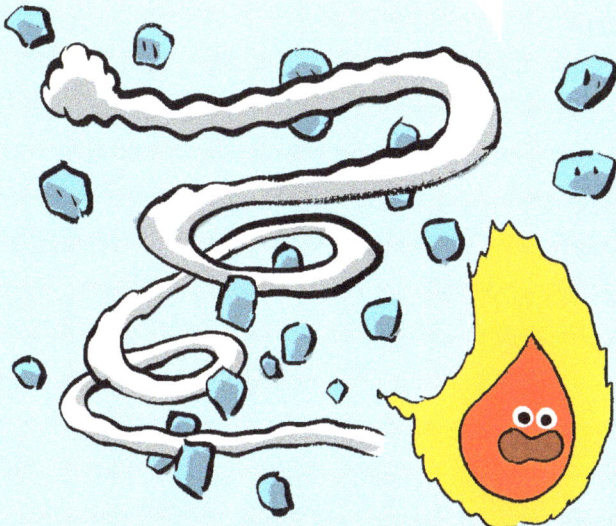

Now, all of the water particles in the glass are moving at the same **speed!**

Most solids and liquids **expand** when they are heated.

They get bigger.

This road is made of asphalt.

On a really hot day, the asphalt expands!

On a cold night, the particles of asphalt become smaller.

That's because most solids and liquids **contract** when they lose me!

16

As the particles lose thermal energy, they move closer together.

smoosh

This process of expansion and contraction causes the road to crack.

Engineers must design all kinds of materials with heat in mind.

Rail lines, bridges, buildings, and even electronics are made to withstand changes in temperature.

Temperature is a measure of the thermal energy in an object.

Glass **thermometers** use expansion and contraction to measure temperature.

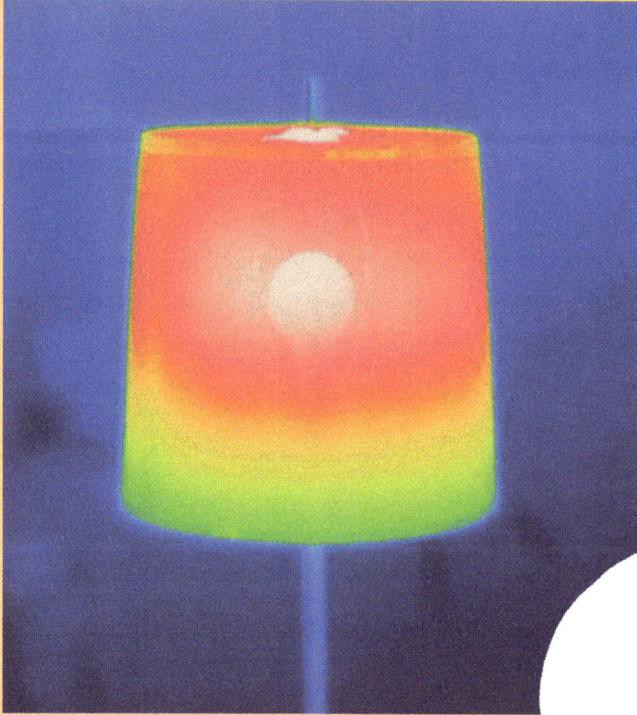

A glass thermometer is filled with a liquid.

When you measure the temperature of something hot, the liquid inside the tube gets heated. It expands and rises.

Keesh

When you measure the temperature of something cold, the liquid contracts. It moves down the tube.

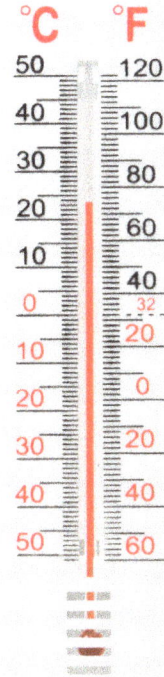

People use thermometers to measure temperature every day. How do you know what kind of clothes to wear?

You measure the temperature outside!

Heating matter can cause it to change physically.

The matter may look different, but it's still made of the same materials.

Take this ice sculpture...

When heat is applied to ice, it melts. It becomes liquid water.

PiP PiP PiP

And when the liquid water is heated, it changes into **water vapor,** a gas. It is still water, just in a different state.

Metals also melt if they are heated to high temperatures.

Sag

This is how we can shape and mold metals into objects.

Heat is always on the move, but I don't always move the same way.

Sometimes I move from particle to particle, much like dominoes tipping over. This allows me to travel through a material.

TIP

The movement of heat from one particle to another is called **conduction.**

CONDUCTION

Solids are often heated by conduction. The particles in solids don't move around freely.

Thermal energy causes them to vibrate in place and bump into nearby particles.

If you leave a metal spoon in a hot pot of food, BEWARE!

The entire spoon will heat up!

The hot food heats up the tip of the spoon...

Then hot particles in the tip of the spoon shake faster and bump into the particles next to them. This transfers thermal energy.

These particles then bump into other particles.

This is how heat moves up the spoon's handle.

Heat also uses particles to travel through liquids and gases.

But unlike solids, the particles of liquids and gases can move around more freely.

They can carry heat around with them as they move about.

In a pot of boiling water, heated water at the bottom of the pot expands.

It rises to the top, forcing the cooler water to the bottom. Then the cooler water becomes warm and rises.

This movement of heat is called **convection**. Convection acts like a conveyor belt to move heat from one place to another.

CONVECTION

Some kinds of heat can travel through empty space.

The movement of heat without any matter to carry it is called **radiation**.

RADIATION

Heat from the sun travels through space to warm Earth.

Heat can also be transferred by radiation where matter is present.

'sup?

You can feel the warmth of a nearby fire even if the air is still. Heat from the fire can travel to your skin by radiation.

Some materials help heat to move easily between objects.

They're called **conductors**.

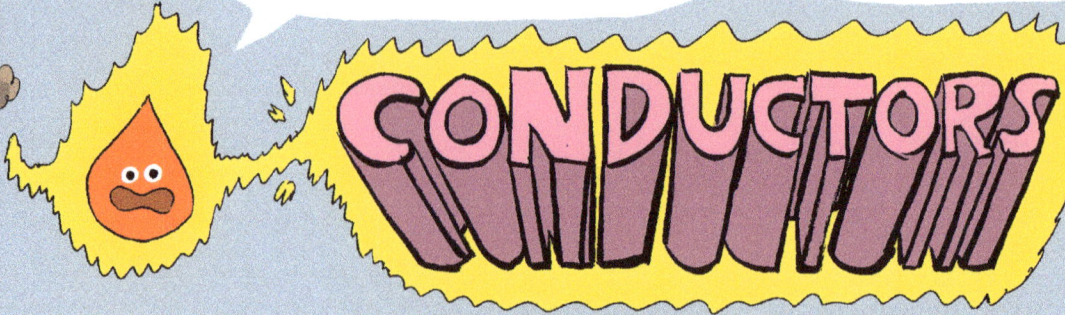

CONDUCTORS

Metals are good conductors. I can travel through this pan very easily!

Insulators are materials that reduce the **motion** of heat.

INSULATORS

You need an insulator to touch a hot pan.

This oven mitt works great!

A winter jacket is another good insulator.

Winter jackets are made of materials like cotton, nylon, and down feathers.

These materials are insulators.

POOF

They do not conduct much heat away from your body.

Some jackets keep wind from stealing heat away from your body.

Wind carries heat away by convection.

WOOSH

Your home is like a big winter jacket.

Its walls are packed with insulation to keep heat in on cold days and out on hot days.

Buildings and other structures would crumble to the ground if they were made with no account for different temperatures.

If your jacket were made of a conductor instead of an insulator, you'd freeze!

BRRR!

BRRR!

If this pot were made of an insulator instead of a conductor, the food would heat up very slowly!
If it were made out of wood, it would burn up!
As long as you're careful, you can use your new knowledge of heat to do amazing things!
What are you waiting for?!

TIMELINE

French scientist Antoine Lavoisier proved that fire is the rapid union of oxygen with other substances.

1777

British scientist James Joule found that heat and energy are interchangeable at a fixed rate.

1847

COLD

1848

1798

American-born scientist Benjamin Thompson stated that the motion of particles in a substance produced heat.

1847

German scientist Hermann von Helmholtz stated that heat is a form of energy.

British scientist Lord Kelvin created a temperature scale with the starting point at absolute zero.

Scottish scientist James Clerk Maxwell published his *Theory of Heat*, in which he describes the fundamentals of thermodynamics.

1871

Death Valley in California, USA, reached 134 °F (57 °C), the highest official recorded natural temperature on Earth.

1913

Astronomers announced the discovery of the hottest known planet that orbits another star. The surface of KELT-9b reaches 7800 °F (4300 °C).

2020

1983

1902

Air conditioning systems for large buildings were introduced.

The coldest directly measured natural temperature on Earth was recorded at Lake Vostok, Antarctica, where the thermometer reached -128.6 °F (-89.2 °C).

WHO'S WHO: LORD KELVIN

Remember that temperature is a measure of the thermal energy of an object. But, can an object have no thermal energy?

That would mean the tiny particles that make up the object have no movement at all!

I have so much laboratory work that I am constantly standing and walking about. I can seldom sit down to write anything!

You sure seem to have a lot of energy! Who are you?

I'm Lord Kelvin. I've been trying to calculate the coldest temperature possible, where all thermal energy is absent. So far, I have calculated this temperature to be -273 degrees on the Celsius scale.

Instead of setting the start of the scale at the freezing point of water as the Celsius temperature scale does, I want my temperature scale to start at the absolute beginning!

Like an **"absolute zero,"** right?

That's catchy! Do you mind if I use that?

By all means!

Fact File

Name: William Thomson (Lord Kelvin)

Born: 1824 in Belfast, Northern Ireland

Occupation: Physicist

Claim to fame: In 1848, he created a temperature scale that begins at absolute zero (-273.15 °C, or -459.67 °F). This scale is known as the *Kelvin scale.*

ACTIVITY: I'M MELTING!

What You'll Need
- Different flat materials, such as a ceramic plate, plastic plate, steel pot, copper pot, or wooden bowl
- Pen and paper
- Ice cubes

Want to learn how different materials conduct heat at different rates?

Gather several flat surfaces made from different materials, such as a ceramic plate, plastic plate, steel pot, or wooden bowl.

Take several ice cubes that are about the same size and put one on each surface. Let them sit undisturbed and watch as the ice melts.

What happened?

Ice needs heat to melt. Some heat will come from the surface it is on. Ice will melt faster on a surface that is a good conductor of heat and slower on a surface that is not a good conductor.

Which materials were the best conductors of heat? Which were the best insulators?

CAN YOU BELIEVE IT?!

There are about 20 different kinds of **water ice.**

Earth's ice is just one kind, but others can form at different temperatures and pressures.

If you're outside on a hot day and want to cool off a drink quickly, wrap a wet paper towel around it. The evaporation of the water from the towel will **cool down the drink.**

Lightning can be as hot as 55,000 °F (30,000 °C)!

The planet **Mercury** reaches 840 °F (450 °C) during the day. But there's **no atmosphere** for heat to spread. So at night, the temperature drops as low as -275 °F (-170 °C).

The color of fire tells you how hot it is! The coolest flame is red, followed by orange, then white. Blue flame is the **hottest.**

HOT

An average **campfire** is about 930 °F (498.9 °C).

Nothing can get colder

than –459.67 °F (–273.15 °C). This temperature is called **absolute zero.**

COLD

Friction,

the property that makes two objects resist moving across one another, also produces heat.

The coolest lava

on Earth erupts from a volcano in Tanzania. The lava is as cool as 930 °F (500 °C).

The average normal

human body

temperature is 98.6 °F (37 °C).

Keesh

All gases and most liquids and solids

expand

when heated. But they do not expand equally.

The part of

the sun

that we see has a temperature of about 10,000 °F (5500 °C)

Only a

tiny fraction

of the heat given off by the sun strikes Earth. Yet it provides the warmth that keeps us—and all other living things on Earth—alive.

The sun's atmosphere, called the corona, is

thousands of degrees hotter

than its surface.

38

WORDS TO KNOW

absolute zero the temperature at which atoms and molecules have the least amount of heat possible.

chemical change a change in which one substance is converted into one or more substances with different properties.

conduction the movement of heat through a material.

conductor something that allows heat, electricity, light, sound, or another form of energy to pass through it.

contract to decrease in size.

convection the transfer of heat by the movement of gas or liquid.

engineer a person who plans and builds engines, machines, roads, bridges, canals, forts, or the like.

expand to increase in size.

insulator something that prevents the passage of electricity, heat, or sound.

matter what all things are made of.

metal any of a large group of elements that includes copper, gold, iron, lead, silver, tin, and other elements that share similar qualities.

motion a change in position.

physical change a change in which matter changes shape or form.

radiation energy given off as waves or small bits of matter. Heat from the sun is one example of radiation.

speed the distance traveled in a certain time.

thermal energy the force that makes particles of matter vibrate and move.

thermometer a tool for measuring temperature.

water vapor water in the state of a gas.

INDEX

www.ingramcontent.com/pod-product-compliance
Lightning Source LLC
Chambersburg PA
CBHW061411090426
42741CB00021B/3484